United States Government Accountability Office

Report to Congressional Requesters

I0425917

February 2012

OIL AND GAS

Interior Has Strengthened Its Oversight of Subsea Well Containment, but Should Improve Its Documentation

GAO

Accountability ★ Integrity ★ Reliability

GAO-12-244

GAO
Accountability * Integrity * Reliability

Highlights

Highlights of GAO-12-244, a report to congressional requesters

OIL AND GAS

Interior Has Strengthened Its Oversight of Subsea Well Containment, but Should Improve Its Documentation

Why GAO Did This Study

On April 20, 2010, an explosion and fire on board the *Deepwater Horizon*, an offshore drilling rig, resulted in 11 deaths and the largest oil spill in U.S. history in the Gulf of Mexico. After this event, the Department of the Interior (Interior), which oversees oil and gas operations in federal waters, suspended certain offshore drilling operations. After developing new guidance, Interior resumed approving drilling operations in the Gulf of Mexico. GAO was asked to examine (1) the industry's improved capabilities for containing subsea wells (those on the ocean floor) in the Gulf of Mexico; (2) Interior's oversight of subsea well containment in the Gulf of Mexico; and (3) the potential to use similar subsea well containment capabilities in other federal waters, such as those along the Alaskan coast.

GAO reviewed laws, regulations, and guidance; documents from oil and gas operators; and Interior's oversight processes. GAO also interviewed agency officials and industry representatives.

What GAO Recommends

To help ensure that operators can respond effectively to a subsea well blowout, GAO recommends that Interior document a time frame for incorporating well containment response scenarios into unannounced spill drills. In commenting on a draft of this report, Interior concurred with GAO's recommendation.

View GAO-12-244. For more information, contact Madhav Panwar at (202) 512-6228 or panwarm@gao.gov or Frank Rusco at (202) 512-3841 or ruscof@gao.gov.

What GAO Found

Since the *Deepwater Horizon* incident, the oil and gas industry has improved its capabilities to respond to a subsea well blowout—the uncontrolled release of oil or gas from a well on the ocean floor—in the Gulf of Mexico. In particular, operators have formed two new not-for-profit organizations that can quickly make available well containment equipment, services, and expertise. Among the equipment that these organizations can provide are capping stacks—devices used to stop the flow of oil or gas from a well. This improved well containment response equipment consists primarily of existing technologies that have been modified to support well containment, according to industry representatives.

Following the *Deepwater Horizon* incident, Interior strengthened its review plans and resources to contain a subsea well blowout; however, its internal oversight processes have not yet been fully documented. Interior has issued guidance to operators outlining information that must be provided to Interior to demonstrate that operators can respond to a well blowout. Interior officials said that they expect to have documentation of their process for reviewing this information in place by spring 2012. Also, Interior incorporated tests of an operator's well containment response capabilities into two unannounced spill drills, and Interior officials told us they intend to incorporate such tests into future spill drills. However, Interior has not documented a time frame for incorporating these tests, and until it does so there is limited assurance of an operator's ability to respond to a subsea well blowout.

Subsea well containment capabilities developed for the Gulf of Mexico could generally be used elsewhere, including Alaskan waters, according to industry representatives and Interior officials. However, because other areas lack the infrastructure and equipment present in the Gulf of Mexico, well blowout response capabilities are more limited. Two operators have submitted plans to Interior to drill in waters north of Alaska as early as the summer of 2012. They are developing, but have not submitted, final well containment plans to Interior, and these plans will need to be approved by Interior before drilling. Oil and gas exploration and production off the coast of Alaska is likely to encounter environmental and logistical risks that differ from those in the Gulf of Mexico because of the region's cold and icy conditions—factors that would also likely affect the response to a well blowout.

A Capping Stack Ready for Deployment

Source: GAO.

_____ **United States Government Accountability Office**

Contents

Abbreviations

BOEM	Bureau of Ocean Energy Management
BOEMRE	Bureau of Ocean Energy Management, Regulation and Enforcement
BSEE	Bureau of Safety and Environmental Enforcement
EPA	Environmental Production Agency
HWCG	Helix Well Containment Group
MMPA	Marine Mammal Protection Act
MWCC	Marine Well Containment Company
ONRR	Office of Natural Resources and Revenue
psig	pounds per square inch

This is a work of the U.S. government and is not subject to copyright protection in the United States. The published product may be reproduced and distributed in its entirety without further permission from GAO. However, because this work may contain copyrighted images or other material, permission from the copyright holder may be necessary if you wish to reproduce this material separately.

United States Government Accountability Office
Washington, DC 20548

February 29, 2012

The Honorable Henry A. Waxman
Ranking Member
Committee on Energy and Commerce
House of Representatives

The Honorable Edward J. Markey
Ranking Member
Committee on Natural Resources
House of Representatives

On April 20, 2010, the *Deepwater Horizon* offshore drilling rig exploded and caught on fire, resulting in 11 deaths, serious injuries, and the largest marine oil spill in the history of the United States. Located over 40 miles off the coast of Louisiana and at a depth of nearly 5,000 feet in the Gulf of Mexico, the subsea well spilled oil for 87 days before responders were able to cap the well and contain the flow of oil. According to government estimates, by that time, over 4.9 million barrels of oil had spilled into the Gulf of Mexico. The spill damaged the environment and adversely affected oil workers and nearby businesses, with estimated costs to compensate for these damages totaling in the billions of dollars.

The nation's economy and security are heavily dependent on oil and natural gas.[1] The Department of the Interior (Interior) regulates oil and gas activities in federal waters, including in the Gulf of Mexico. According to a 2010 Interior study, almost 97 percent of U.S. offshore oil and gas activity in federal waters occurs there. However, drilling for oil and gas is an inherently risky undertaking, and although industry has the capability to respond to subsea blowouts—the uncontrolled release of oil or gas from a well on the ocean floor— the risk of the loss of control of a subsea well can never be entirely eliminated. Given this risk—and the severity of the consequences—it is critical that the operators who lease public lands and the federal agency that oversees them demonstrate that they are taking all reasonable steps to mitigate these risks. Following the *Deepwater Horizon* incident, for example, Interior suspended certain

---

[1]Petroleum exists in both liquid and gaseous forms. Throughout this report, we refer to the liquid forms as "oil" and the gaseous forms as "gas."

GAO-12-244 Subsea Well Containment

offshore drilling operations and developed new regulations and guidance for oil and gas operators. Interior lifted this moratorium on October 12, 2010, and on February 28, 2011, issued its first permit for offshore drilling under the new guidance.

In this context, you asked us to examine Interior's approach to addressing the risk of subsea well blowouts and oversight of industries' well containment capabilities.[2] Our objectives were to examine (1) improvements to subsea well containment capabilities now available for use in the Gulf of Mexico; (2) Interior's oversight of subsea well containment in the Gulf of Mexico following the *Deepwater Horizon* incident; and (3) the potential to use similar subsea well containment capabilities in other federal waters, such as those off the Alaskan coast.

To examine subsea well containment capabilities, we reviewed technical documents that the two well containment organizations that operate in the Gulf of Mexico provided to Interior and visited facilities, both in the United States and in the United Kingdom, where certain well containment equipment was stored, displayed, or tested. In addition, we also interviewed Interior officials to identify the capabilities used to support new applications to drill. We also interviewed representatives of the two well containment organizations to identify capping and containment capabilities and learn how they would deploy and operate these capabilities in a subsea well blowout.[3] For the purposes of this report, we focused on capacities for subsea well containment and did not review surface oil spill response capabilities, such as booms, which are floating barriers serving to contain an oil spill, or oil skimmers, which are devices that separate oil from water. To examine Interior's oversight of subsea well containment, we reviewed laws, regulations, and current guidance that pertain to subsea well control and interviewed agency officials responsible for reviewing and approving well containment plans. We reviewed a nonprobability sample of 7 well containment plans from the over 30 that had been approved by Interior as of August 2011 representing different well characteristics to further understand the

---

[2]"Well containment" refers to measures taken after an event such as a blowout to regain control of the well and capture any released oil.

[3]The Marine Well Containment Company and the Helix Well Containment Group were the two organizations formed after the *Deepwater Horizon* incident to offer well containment services in the Gulf of Mexico.

capabilities and plans for capping and containment.[4] We also interviewed officials from Interior and the oil and gas industry to identify the capabilities that U.S.-based and international organizations use to address subsea well blowouts. To determine the potential to use subsea well containment capabilities available for the Gulf of Mexico in other federal waters, such as those along the Alaskan coast, we reviewed documents and interviewed officials from Interior responsible for permitting in Alaskan waters as well as operators and industry groups.

We conducted this performance audit from April 2011 to January 2012, in accordance with generally accepted government auditing standards. Those standards require that we plan and perform the audit to obtain sufficient, appropriate evidence to provide a reasonable basis for our findings and conclusions based on our audit objectives. We believe that the evidence obtained provides a reasonable basis for our findings and conclusions based on our audit objectives.

Background

According to a 2010 Interior study, 97 percent of oil and gas production in federal waters occurs along the U.S. outer continental shelf of the Gulf of Mexico. The outer continental shelf is the submerged lands outside the territorial jurisdiction of all 50 states but within U.S. jurisdiction and control.[5] The outer continental shelf contains an estimated 85 billion barrels of oil, and over half of this oil is located in the Gulf of Mexico.[6] Significant reserves also exist in the outer continental shelf off Alaska.

Interior is responsible for the oversight of oil and gas activities on the U.S. outer continental shelf, which includes submerged lands in federal waters off the coast of Alaska, in the Gulf of Mexico, and off the Atlantic and

---

[4]Because this was a nonprobability sample, we cannot generalize the information derived from these well containment plans to all such plans; these plans provide examples of plans developed by five different operators and different well depths, ranging from 3,300 to 6,600 feet.

[5]The outer continental shelf consists of submerged federal lands, generally extending seaward between 3 and 200 nautical miles off the coastline.

[6]This estimate is according to a 2006 Interior assessment of technically recoverable resources, not all of which may be economically recoverable.

Pacific coasts.[7] As part of its responsibilities, Interior leases blocks of land in the outer continental shelf for mineral development, including oil and gas exploration and production. The lease holder may operate the well or may hire other companies to perform drilling operations and other related services. Operators submit a series of documents to Interior for approval to drill, including an application for permit to drill and an oil spill response plan. In October 2010, Interior promulgated certain new requirements for the application for permit to drill process designed to prevent a blowout including, among other things, requiring independent third-party verification that the subsea blowout preventer is compatible with the specific well location and well design. The oil spill response plan is to include an operator's proposed methods for ensuring that oil spill containment and recovery equipment and response personnel are mobilized and deployed in the event of a spill. This plan is to be implemented immediately following a spill. The plan is also to include an inventory of spill response resources such as materials and supplies, services, equipment, and response vessels available locally and regionally, as well as a description of the operator's procedures for conducting monthly inspections and necessary maintenance of recovery equipment. As part of its oversight responsibilities, Interior is required to conduct scheduled and unscheduled inspections of offshore facilities, such as drilling rigs and production platforms. Equipment scheduled for inspections includes equipment designed to prevent or alleviate blowouts, fires, spillages, or other major accidents.

Also under its oversight responsibilities, Interior issues guidance called a Notice to Lessees and Operators to clarify, supplement, or provide more detail about certain requirements, including requirements for applications for permit to drill. In response to the *Deepwater Horizon* incident, Interior

---

[7]In April 2010, Interior initiated a reorganization of its bureau responsible for overseeing offshore oil and natural gas activities. Specifically, in May 2010, Interior announced that it would be reorganizing its Minerals Management Service—the bureau previously tasked with overseeing offshore oil and natural gas activities into three separate bureaus: the Bureau of Ocean Energy Management (BOEM), the Bureau of Safety and Environmental Enforcement (BSEE), and the Office of Natural Resources and Revenue (ONRR). In June 2010, Interior announced that the former Minerals Management Service would be known as the Bureau of Ocean Energy Management, Regulation and Enforcement (BOEMRE). Effective October 1, 2010, ONRR became an office under the Interior's Assistant Secretary-Policy, Management and Budget. On October 1, 2011, BOEM—which oversees leasing and resource management, and BSEE, which is responsible for issuing oil and natural gas drilling permits and conducting inspections—began functioning as separate bureaus.

issued a number of these notices, which, among other things, notified operators that Interior would be evaluating whether they had submitted adequate information about their well containment capabilities with their oil spill response plans. Specifically, in a November 2010 notice, Interior informed operators that it would evaluate whether operators could demonstrate that they had access to and could deploy well containment resources that would be adequate to promptly respond to a blowout or other loss of well control. This notice applies only to operators conducting operations using subsea blowout preventers, which are devices placed on wells to help maintain control over pressures in the well, or blowout preventers on floating facilities. Operators provide information on their well containment capabilities to Interior in a collection of documents that compose a well containment plan. According to Interior officials, all approved applications for permit to drill subject to the November 2010 notice have included a well containment plan. For additional information on the types of information operators provide in their well containment plans, see appendix I.

There are three phases to produce oil or gas from a subsea well: drilling, completion, and production. During the drilling phase, operators drill a hole, called the wellbore, from the seafloor down to the reservoir of oil or gas. Early in this phase, a blowout preventer is placed on top of the wellhead, which, in turn, is installed on top of the wellbore to provide an interface between the wellbore and other equipment. A large-diameter pipe called the riser connects the drilling rig to the blowout preventer, and the drill pipe, drill bit, drilling mud, and casing are routed down to the well through the riser and blowout preventer.[8] Industry officials we spoke with said that during the drilling phase, operators must constantly balance the pressure of the drilling mud inside the wellbore with the pressure from the surrounding formation thousands of feet below the seafloor. Interior officials explained that during this phase, operators may encounter a number of unknown well conditions, which if not controlled or corrected could pose a risk of a blowout. During a blowout, operators close the

---

[8]Casing is a metal pipe that is inserted inside the wellbore to prevent high-pressure fluids outside the formation from entering the well, and to prevent drilling mud inside the well from fracturing fragile sections of the wellbore. As drilling progresses with depth, casings that are slightly narrower than the hole created by the drill bit are inserted into the wellbore and bonded in place with cement, sealing the wellbore from the surrounding formation. Drilling mud is special fluid pumped through the wellbore at different densities to maintain a pressure balance inside the wellbore, lubricate the drilling bit, and bring rock and other matter cut from the formation back to the rig.

valves in the blowout preventer in an attempt to seal the wellbore and prevent oil and gas from escaping to the surface. Figure 1 illustrates the drilling phase.

Figure 1: Key Equipment Used during the Drilling Phase

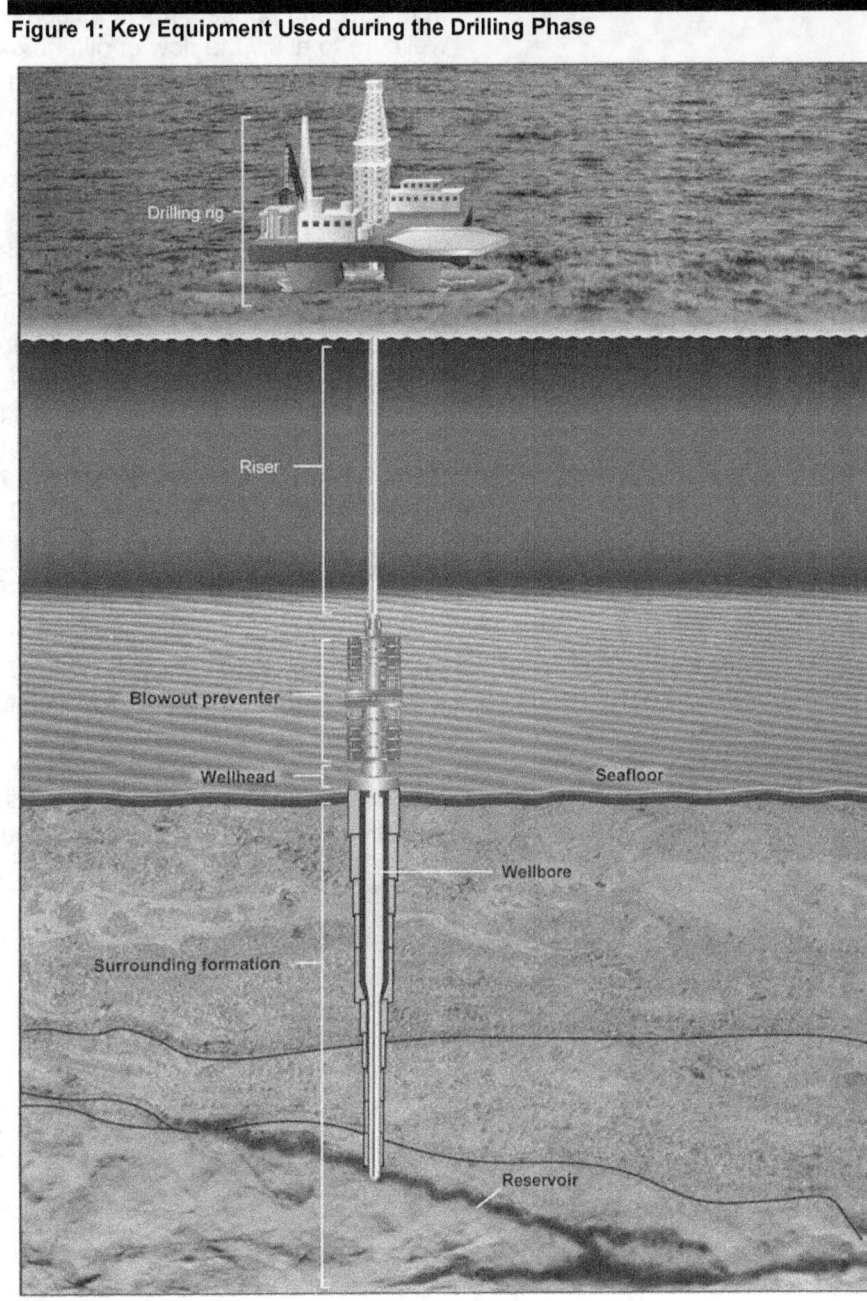

Sources: GAO analysis of industry plans and reports; Art Explosion (photos).

Note: Objects in figure are not to scale.

In the second phase, known as completion, the operator opens the wellbore to allow the flow of oil and gas from the reservoir, and installs equipment at the top of the wellbore to control and collect the oil and gas. The third phase is production, the extraction of oil or gas from the well.[9]

The difficulty of the drilling process can vary depending on the depth of the seafloor as well as the depth of the reservoir. According to a 2010 Interior study, the majority of oil production in the Gulf of Mexico occurs in deep water, which the study defined as 1,000 feet or more below sea level.[10] Deepwater wells tend to produce a relatively large amount of oil and gas compared with wells in shallower water, in part because high reservoir pressures contribute to well productivity. These high pressures also make drilling deepwater wells significantly more dangerous than drilling shallow wells because, among other things, the increased pressure can exacerbate the effects of a blowout and make a well containment response more challenging. In the case of the well that the *Deepwater Horizon* was drilling, the seafloor was nearly 5,000 feet below sea level, and the operator, BP, drilled an additional 13,000 feet below the seafloor to reach the reservoir.

According to several studies of the *Deepwater Horizon* incident, drilling had already been completed when high-pressure oil and gas unexpectedly breached a cement barrier placed inside the wellbore. This allowed oil and gas to flow unimpeded up the riser to the *Deepwater Horizon* drilling rig on the surface, resulting in an explosion.[11] As a result, the *Deepwater Horizon* drilling rig caught fire and sank roughly 36 hours later. Over the next 87 days, BP made numerous attempts to stop the flow of oil from the well but was unsuccessful until it installed a capping stack, a device similar to but generally smaller than a blowout preventer

---

[9]Before the production phase begins, the blowout preventer is removed to allow installation of equipment for producing oil or gas.

[10]According to a 2011 report by the National Commission on the BP *Deepwater Horizon* Oil Spill and Offshore Drilling, companies and governmental organizations have adopted definitions for deepwater ranging from 600 to 1,500 feet.

[11]The crew of the *Deepwater Horizon* drilling rig attempted to stop the flow of oil and gas by closing the blowout preventer after the fluids had entered the riser, but this failed to seal the well.

GAO-12-244 Subsea Well Containment

that is specifically designed to cap a well after a blowout.[12] While the blowout preventer is designed to manage drilling operations and prevent a blowout, a capping stack is designed to be deployed after a subsea blowout has already occurred. At the time of the *Deepwater Horizon* incident, there were few capping stacks in existence, and capabilities to support subsea well containment were limited.

Industry Has Improved Its Capabilities for Subsea Well Containment in the Gulf of Mexico

Since the *Deepwater Horizon* incident, the oil and gas industry has improved its capabilities to respond to a subsea well blowout in the Gulf of Mexico. In particular, operators have formed two new organizations that are expected to offer improved well containment capabilities, including more effective equipment and services, and expertise to member operators in the event of a well blowout. The subsea well containment capabilities available for the Gulf of Mexico consist primarily of existing technologies that have been modified to support well containment.

Two Industry Organizations Provide Subsea Well Containment in the Gulf of Mexico

Following the *Deepwater Horizon* incident, two not-for-profit organizations of oil and gas companies—the Marine Well Containment Company (MWCC) and the Helix Well Containment Group (HWCG)—formed to provide subsea well containment capabilities and support to operators in the Gulf of Mexico that enter into contracts with them. Once under contract and in the event of a spill, each of these well containment organizations is to provide certain containment equipment and services—capping stacks, vessels, and other resources necessary to respond to a subsea blowout—that operators can customize to their well containment needs. Equipment and services provided by these well containment organizations were developed in consultation with Interior and have been a key part of the well containment plans that operators submit to Interior, according to Interior officials. All of the operators subject to Interior's November 2010 notice that have received permission to drill in the Gulf of Mexico since the moratorium was lifted have contracted with one or both

---

[12]According to a 2011 report by the National Commission on the BP *Deepwater Horizon* Oil Spill and Offshore Drilling, the well was closed permanently when BP drilled a relief well that intersected the problem well and then pumped concrete into the problem well to seal the wellbore. Interior also published a Drilling Safety Rule in October 2010 that included provisions intended to help improve blowout prevention practices in order to enhance the safety of oil and gas drilling operations.

of these well containment organizations to provide certain well containment equipment and resources in the event of a subsea blowout, according to these officials.

In general, MWCC members include some of the largest operators with oil and gas exploration and production activities in the Gulf of Mexico, such as ExxonMobil, ConocoPhillips, Chevron, and Shell, and HWCG members include operators of various sizes. Some operators are members of both groups. More specifically:

- MWCC operates as an independent, stand-alone company where each of its 10 members has equal ownership and voting rights, and according to MWCC representatives, its members drilled approximately 70 percent of deepwater wells drilled in the U.S. Gulf of Mexico from 2007 through 2009.

- HWCG is a consortium of 24 operators, which, according to HWCG representatives, represent approximately 80 percent of the deepwater operators in the Gulf of Mexico. HWCG was created around the well containment capabilities offered by one deepwater services company whose equipment was used in the response to the *Deepwater Horizon incident.*

According to representatives from both well containment organizations, members also commit to mutual aid agreements in which operators agree to provide equipment or other support to consortium members that experience a subsea well blowout. Representatives of the well containment organizations said that both HWCG and MWCC also offer services to nonmembers on a fee basis. Furthermore, representatives of the well containment organizations we spoke with generally agreed that should another incident like *Deepwater Horizon* occur, industry would mobilize to make available all of the equipment and services necessary to ensure a quick and effective response.

In addition to equipment and services, both MWCC and HWCG provide overall plans that identify how the equipment and services are to be deployed and used; a schedule of activities to be followed; various contingencies for high-risk activities, such as straightening a bent wellhead that may have been damaged by a blowout; and names and contact information for technical experts who may be called on as required. According to Interior officials, operators would need to customize the well containment organizations' overall plans to their specific well design. For example, the well pressure would determine the specifications of the capping stack, and the depth of the well would specify which ships have cables long enough to reach it. These customized plans comprise some of the documents in the well containment plans that operators submit to Interior. However, operators may need additional equipment and services that the well containment organizations do not provide. For example, the well containment organizations provide capping stacks for well containment, but in some— if not all—cases the operator must identify a separate service provider to transport the capping stack to the site and deploy it to the well. In their well containment plans, operators also identify other needed equipment and services that may not be provided by the well containment organization, including debris removal equipment, remotely operated underwater vehicles, which are controlled from surface vessels and used to, among other things, clear debris, and apply chemicals called dispersants that are used to disperse leaked oil.

Subsea Well Containment Capabilities Available for the Gulf of Mexico Consist Primarily of Modifications to Established Technologies

The subsea well containment capabilities that MWCC and HWCG offer for the Gulf of Mexico consist primarily of established technologies that have been modified to support well containment. For example, according to industry representatives, capping stacks are devices similar to previously used blowout preventers and contain many of the same components. According to representatives from the two well containment organizations, the well containment capabilities (i.e., equipment, procedures, and processes that MWCC and HWCG would activate in the event of a subsea blowout in the Gulf of Mexico) incorporate established technologies commonly used for offshore well drilling. Well containment capabilities in the Gulf of Mexico include the following:

- containment equipment, including capping stacks used to shut in a well, and containment domes and top hats that are used to collect escaping oil and gas and flow them to the surface;[13]

- subsea support systems, such as riser systems that direct captured oil and gas to surface vessels in the event that the well cannot be shut in completely; utility equipment, such as dispersant injection systems,

---

[13]Containment domes and top hats are devices used to collect oil and gas in a subsea environment, but their use may be limited under some conditions because hydrocarbons can freeze and form hydrates that clog the devices' collection tubes.

hydrate inhibitor systems, and hydraulic power systems; manifolds and connection systems; and remotely operated vehicles;[14] and

- surface vessels, such as multipurpose containment response vessels that can be configured to conduct a variety of drilling or containment activities, production vessels that can process captured oil, storage tankers to transport the captured oil, and other support vessels used to distribute dispersants and control remotely operated underwater vehicles.

Figure 2 illustrates a subsea well containment response system.

---

[14]A dispersant is used on the surface and subsea to break up oil and gas into smaller particles, making it easier for microorganisms to consume the oil and making it less hazardous to responding personnel on the surface. Hydrate inhibitors help in preventing subsea oil from freezing up and forming hydrates that can clog tubes that collect and route oil and gas to the surface. Hydraulic power systems are situated on the seafloor and provide power for remotely operated vehicles and other equipment on the seafloor. Manifolds are used to control fluid flow. Remotely operated underwater vehicles are controlled from surface vessels and are used to show the debris field, clear debris, and activate functions on the blowout preventer and capping stack.

Figure 2: Subsea Well Containment Response Equipment

Source: GAO analysis of industry plans and reports; photos Art Explosion.

Note: Objects in figure are not to scale.

A key component of both MWCC and HWCG's response capability is a capping stack. According to industry representatives, capping stacks are essentially lighter, specialized versions of blowout preventers that use similar components to stop or control the flow of oil and gas. The capping stacks built for MWCC and HWCG are designed to withstand the high pressures experienced in deepwater reservoirs—up to 15,000 pounds per square inch for the most recent capping stacks. These stacks can be deployed to 10,000 feet below sea level. Most capping stacks have multiple outlets that allow oil and gas to be routed to surface vessels and processed. Capping stacks are usually deployed on top of the blowout preventer but can also be installed on other points, including the wellhead. Industry representatives told us that fittings between connection points are generally standardized but that capping stacks can be modified with different fittings to allow for proper installation. Once a capping stack is installed, depending on the scenario, the containment plans typically call for slowly closing each of the outlets until the well is closed. In some cases, operators may also be able to deploy dispersants into or around the capping stack to help break up the oil (see fig. 3).[15]

---

[15]GAO is currently conducting work looking at what is known about the use of dispersants, efforts by federal agencies and other stakeholders to enhance knowledge on the use of dispersants and their effects, and the challenges researchers face in doing so.

Figure 3: A Capping Stack Ready for Deployment

Source: GAO.

Capping stacks are a primary component of HWCG and MWCC well containment capabilities, but Interior officials told us that it does not require operators to use any particular technology in the Gulf of Mexico. Instead, Interior expects operators to demonstrate that they have the capability to control a well with a capping stack or some other functionally equivalent technology, and according to Interior officials, capping stacks have demonstrated that capability. Industry representatives told us that capping stacks are tested periodically and physically located near staging points around the Gulf of Mexico, where they can be moved offshore rapidly. When not needed, they are stored onshore and not used for any other purpose. Representatives from both HWCG and MWCC told us that both of their organizations have multiple capping stacks ready for deployment.

In addition to capping stacks, well containment capabilities rely on other equipment and services to transport the capping stack to the well site, assist with debris removal, and collect oil and gas from the capping stack.[16] This equipment includes surface vessels that can collect oil and gas from the capping stack or other collection devices, vessels with lift and hoist capabilities to position and move the capping stack, control ships with electronics to monitor the pressures and status of the capping stack, and remotely operated vehicles that perform a variety of subsea operations. In their well containment plans, operators provide Interior with a list of this other equipment as well as how it could be utilized and positioned at the blowout location.

Interior Has Issued New Guidance and Is Documenting Many of Its Oversight Processes, but Has Not Documented a Time Frame for Testing Operators' Responses to a Subsea Blowout

Following the *Deepwater Horizon* incident, Interior issued new guidance that identified information operators are to provide to demonstrate well containment capability, but Interior has not fully documented its internal process for reviewing this information. Also, the well containment plans that operators submit to Interior as part of the permitting process identify equipment, such as a capping stack, that would be needed for well containment response, but Interior has not yet documented its process for ensuring that this equipment is regularly inspected and available. Finally, while Interior has conducted two unannounced spill drills that incorporated scenarios for well containment, it has not documented a time frame for incorporating these tests in the future.

Interior Issued New Guidance and Is Documenting a Process for Providing Oversight

Interior issued guidance following the *Deepwater Horizon* incident that identifies information that operators are to provide to demonstrate they can respond adequately and promptly to a blowout or other loss of well control, but the agency has not documented its process for reviewing the information it receives. A Notice to Lessees and Operators issued on November 8, 2010, after *Deepwater Horizon,* identifies specific information, including types of well containment equipment accessible to the operator in the event of a spill, that operators are to provide to Interior to ensure that operators' spill response plans are adequate. Interior issued subsequent supplemental guidance on the November 2010 notice

---

[16]The riser between the drilling rig and the wellhead can collapse after a blowout and may create a large debris field on top of the well that the operator must clear before proceeding.

on December 13, 2010, explaining that it would review this information as part of the application for permit to drill approval process. For example, operators are to provide information describing their plans to use capping stacks; containment domes; subsea utility equipment, including hydraulic power, hydrate control, and dispersant systems; riser systems; remotely operated underwater vehicles; and oil collection vessels. Operators may satisfy these new information requirements by submitting a well containment plan as part of their oil spill response plans.

Interior officials told us that they discuss their expectations for the contents of these plans with individual operators but noted that the agency has not finalized documentation of these expectations or completed the documentation of its internal process for reviewing these plans. Interior officials who review these plans have developed a one-page checklist outlining the types of information they review, but the checklist does not provide criteria for assessing the information. For example, the checklist asks "Does the plan adequately address debris removal?" but does not provide criteria for determining whether the information the operator included is adequate. These officials said they are in the process of documenting their review process and expect to have the documentation in place by spring 2012.

Under the *Standards for Internal Control in the Federal Government*, federal agencies are to employ control activities, such as to clearly document internal control in management directives, administrative policies, or operating manuals, and the documentation is to be readily available for examination.[17] Interior officials told us that the agency plans to transfer the responsibility for reviewing well containment plans to another office in 2012, and will document the review process before that time. In the meantime, Interior officials told us that they rely on the expertise and judgment of staff to perform these reviews and communicate their expectations to operators. Until the agency completes a documented review process, Interior cannot provide reasonable assurance that well containment plans will be reviewed consistently.

---

[17]See GAO, *Standards for Internal Control in the Federal Government*, GAO/AIMD-00-21.3.1 (Washington, D.C.: November 1999). These standards, issued pursuant to the requirements of the Federal Managers' Financial Integrity Act of 1982, provide the overall framework for establishing and maintaining internal control in the federal government.

In addition to the new guidance issued since the *Deepwater Horizon* incident, as part of Interior's review of well containment plans, Interior and operators use a new software tool to analyze a proposed well's design and its ability to withstand increased pressures that result when an uncontrolled well is closed by a capping stack. In certain situations, capping the well shut could cause portions of the well to burst, potentially allowing oil and gas to flow up through the seabed and releasing oil and gas into the sea from outside the wellbore. This new software tool, called the well containment screening tool, helps Interior and operators evaluate whether a well could be closed using a capping stack and still maintain wellbore integrity. The development of this screening tool was initiated by Interior and completed with input from the oil industry. The screening tool analyzes potential well integrity and risk based on various factors including well design, geological characteristics, reservoir pressures, and wellbore fluid gradients. Interior provides the tool to operators and then reviews each operator's analysis of expected wellbore integrity; following this review, Interior may advise operators to adjust screening tool parameters when appropriate. According to Interior officials, on at least 12 occasions, an operator strengthened its wellbore design based on the results of the screening tool. Industry representatives we met with also said that the screening tool was valuable for helping address the risks associated with a subsea blowout by requiring operators to document their well design decisions and have those decisions reviewed by Interior. According to Interior officials, in some cases, Interior may have access to a wider set of data on the geological characteristics of the area than the operator. In these cases, Interior can advise the operator on the need to modify its well design.

Interior Is Documenting Its Process to Ensure Equipment Is Inspected and Available, but Has Not Documented a Time Frame for Incorporating Well Containment Scenarios into Unannounced Spill Drills

As previously stated in this report, since the *Deepwater Horizon* incident, the well containment plans that operators submit to Interior as part of the permitting process identify equipment that the operator plans to use to contain subsea well blowouts. However, Interior does not have a fully documented process and associated schedule to ensure that the equipment is regularly inspected and available for deployment. Interior regulations that have been in place since before the *Deepwater Horizon* spill specify that operators are to submit an oil spill response plan that identifies procedures the operator is to follow in the event of a spill, including methods to ensure the availability of oil spill response equipment and an inventory of this equipment and the operator's procedures for conducting monthly inspections. Interior is also required to conduct inspections of offshore facilities and response equipment. Interior has scheduled inspections of surface response equipment but has not scheduled regular inspections of well containment equipment. Interior officials we met with told us that they have observed officials from the well containment organizations conducting certain tests of all capping stacks identified in well containment plans approved for the Gulf of Mexico.[18] These tests include pressure tests to ensure that the capping stack can withstand well pressures, and functional tests to ensure that components operate properly. However, Interior officials told us that the agency does not have a regular schedule for inspecting such equipment and does not specify what tests should be conducted to ensure that the equipment is in operational condition. The officials added that by June 2012 Interior plans to have a process that (1) establishes a schedule for testing equipment and (2) identifies the tests that will be conducted as part of the agency's oversight of operator readiness to respond to a subsea event.

While Interior does not have a documented process for monitoring the availability of equipment that operators identify in their well containment plans, this concern is somewhat mitigated by the number of vessels and capping stacks located in the Gulf of Mexico that could aid a well containment response in the event that dedicated equipment is unavailable. Interior officials told us that they expect well containment plans to list multiple replacement vessels and equipment to demonstrate this redundancy, and these officials believe this sufficiently mitigates the possibility that resources could be unavailable in the event of a subsea blowout. In addition, Interior relies on operators to inform them when well containment equipment is unavailable, and industry representatives told us that the two well containment organizations are to inform their members and Interior when critical equipment is out of service.

In addition, Interior has not determined the extent to which it will conduct drills to test operators' abilities to respond to a subsea well blowout. Interior's regulations provide for periodic unannounced drills to test the spill response preparedness of operators, but Interior has not set a time frame for incorporating well containment scenarios into these exercises that would test operators' abilities to implement their well containment plans. Interior conducts these drills to, among other things, test an operator's ability to notify the appropriate entities and personnel in the

---

[18]Although not explicitly required by Interior, capping stacks have been included in all well containment plans that have been approved by Interior. Interior officials told us that it does not require capping stacks as part of the well containment plan because it does not want to limit industry's use of alternative technologies to contain well blowouts.

event of a spill, including federal regulatory agencies, affected state and local agencies, internal response coordinators, and response contractors, and to take appropriate action to implement the operator's response plan. If the decisions made during the drill do not align with the approved oil spill response plan, the drill provides an opportunity to determine what needs to change in the response process. In September 2011, Interior conducted its first unannounced spill drill that included a subsea well containment scenario, and held a second unannounced drill in December 2011. According to Interior officials, the agency plans to incorporate subsea well containment scenarios in certain future unannounced spill drills with operators. According to these officials, Interior staff have observed well containment exercises conducted by the two well containment organizations in the Gulf of Mexico. However, Interior has not tested most operators' ability to respond to a subsea blowout, and has not established a time frame to incorporate these tests into unannounced spill drills. Until Interior sets a time frame for incorporating well containment scenarios into unannounced spill drills, there is limited assurance that operators are prepared to respond to a subsea blowout.

Subsea Well Containment Capabilities Available for the Gulf of Mexico Could Be Used in Other Federal Waters, but Environmental and Logistical Risks Differ

Subsea well containment capabilities similar to what industry offers for the Gulf of Mexico could generally be used in other federal waters, including the outer continental shelf off Alaska. Industry officials said that they are developing a well containment response capability for use in this region. Moreover, operators of subsea wells off the Alaskan coast are likely to face operating conditions that pose different environmental and logistical risks than those faced in the Gulf of Mexico and may require modified blowout response plans.

Capabilities Available for the Gulf of Mexico Could Be Used in Other Regions

According to industry representatives and Interior officials we spoke with, capping stacks and other equipment available to respond to blowouts in the Gulf of Mexico could be used in other federal waters. For example, because capping stacks are installed on top of the wellhead or blowout preventer, they are not affected by the condition of the seafloor, so they could be used in other regions. Industry representatives explained that the connection points between subsea devices like wellheads, blowout preventers, and capping stacks are mostly standardized and that these connections can be exchanged on a capping stack to ensure a proper fit.[19] Capping stacks may be specialized for particular regions, but Interior officials and industry representatives told us that capping stacks developed for use in the Arctic would not need to manage the same pressures as capping stacks developed for use in the Gulf of Mexico because reservoir pressures in the Gulf of Mexico are generally much higher.

Industry Is Developing Well Containment Capabilities for the Alaska Outer Continental Shelf

For the past two decades, the majority of subsea oil and gas exploration and production in U.S. waters has occurred in the Gulf of Mexico; however, in 2010, Shell Oil submitted plans to Interior to drill in the waters north of Alaska as early as the summer of 2012.[20] In August 2011, Interior conditionally gave approval to Shell Oil to drill exploratory wells along the north shore of Alaska in the Beaufort Sea, pending receipt and approval of Shell's well containment plans and other requirements.[21] In December 2011, Interior conditionally gave approval to Shell to drill in the Chukchi Sea, again pending receipt and approval of Shell's well containment plans and other requirements.[22] If Shell submits these materials to Interior and Interior approves them, Shell could begin drilling in these areas early as the summer of 2012. Figure 4 illustrates the location of the Beaufort and Chukchi Seas relative to Alaska and the Arctic Circle.

---

[19]Interior officials told us that they expect operators that use a capping stack as part of a well containment response plan to demonstrate to Interior that the capping stack can be attached to each of the potential connection points on an uncontrolled well.

[20]In August 2011, ConocoPhillips submitted a draft exploration plan for the Chukchi Sea.

[21]Interior's approval is also subject to a petition for review by environmental groups. *Petition at 2, Native Village of Point Hope, et. al. v. Salazar, et. al.*, No. 11-72891 (9th Cir. filed Sept. 29, 2011). Environmental groups have also challenged a permit issued by the Environmental Protection Agency (EPA) to Shell under the Clean Air Act for emissions from the *Kulluk* drilling unit and vessels that Shell proposes to use for exploratory drilling in the Beaufort Sea. That challenge is currently pending in front of EPA's Environmental Appeals Board.

[22]One condition of Interior's approval for exploratory drilling in both the Beaufort and Chukchi Seas is Shell's receipt of an approved Marine Mammal Protection Act (MMPA) authorization and Interior's receipt of a corresponding Endangered Species Act Incidental Take Statement. The National Oceanic and Atmospheric Administration released a draft environmental impact statement exploring these points in December 2011.

Figure 4: The Beaufort and Chukchi Seas off the Coast of Alaska

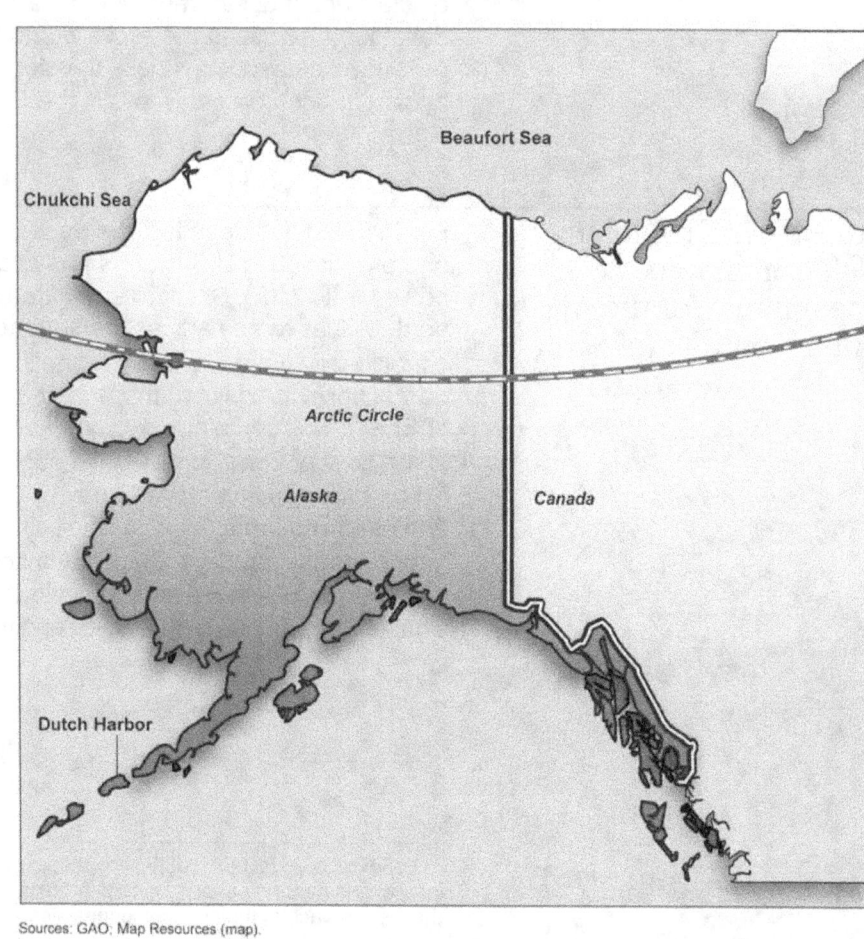

Sources: GAO; Map Resources (map).

According to Shell representatives, the company is still developing the capabilities that it will need to support well containment operations in the Beaufort and Chukchi Seas. These capabilities are to include a capping stack similar in design and functionality to capping stacks already inspected and approved for use in the Gulf of Mexico.[23] Shell's capping stack has been specifically designed for use in Arctic waters and,

---

[23]Trendsetter Engineering built capping stacks for MWCC and HWCG and is designing and fabricating Shell's capping stack.

according to Shell representatives, is expected to be completed by April 2012.

According to Shell representatives we spoke with, Shell is to have dedicated capping and containment capabilities at sea and ready for deployment. In the event of a subsea well blowout, Shell will deploy a capping stack as its primary response. The capping stack is to be housed on an icebreaking vessel supporting drilling operations in the Beaufort Sea, according to the Shell representatives.[24] The icebreaking vessel is to have the lifting capability to deploy the stack onto an uncontrolled well. Shell representatives said that if a blowout occurred on a well in the Chukchi Sea, operations in the Beaufort Sea would be shut down and the icebreaking vessel with the capping stack and other supporting vessels would be deployed from the Beaufort Sea to the Chukchi Sea.[25] Likewise, in the event of a well blowout in the Beaufort Sea, Shell would cease operations in the Chukchi Sea and send support vessels to assist operations in the Beaufort Sea.[26]

Alaska's Operating Conditions Pose Risks to Subsea Well Containment

Subsea drilling operations in Alaska will face operating conditions that greatly differ from those in the Gulf of Mexico and may pose unique risks. For example, the Beaufort and Chukchi Seas are inside the Arctic Circle, with cold and icy conditions for much of the year and with few daylight hours during the winter. Interior and Coast Guard officials said that a well containment response in Alaskan waters might face certain risks that could delay or impede a response to a blowout.[27] For example, if a

---

[24]According to Shell officials, Shell has contracted with a Finnish company to provide the icebreaking vessels *Nordica* and *Fennica* to support operations in the Beaufort and Chukchi Seas.

[25]In the event of a subsea well blowout, the drilling rig could become disabled. According to Shell documents, in such an event the drilling rig at the other site would be required to drill relief wells at the blowout site.

[26]Chukchi Sea operations would also include an icebreaking vessel but without the capping stack.

[27]Shell representatives told us that the prospects in some areas of the Beaufort and Chukchi Seas pose less risk than prospects for some wells in the Gulf of Mexico because the wells in Alaska will be situated 100 to 150 feet below the surface, would generally have much lower reservoir pressures, and the rate at which oil and gas would flow from a well blowout would be much lower than the rate for wells drilled in deeper waters in the Gulf of Mexico.

blowout were to occur at the end of the drilling season in late October, surface ice and temperatures could pose risks to a well containment response.[28]

Even with Shell's plans to have dedicated capping stack and well containment capabilities in the region to provide rapid response in the event of a blowout, these dedicated capabilities do not completely mitigate some of the environmental and logistical risks associated with the remoteness and environment of the region. Environmental challenges include the following:

- *Surface ice.* According to Interior officials, Shell proposes to drill from July 15 through October 31, except for a period in late August to allow for whale hunting by the indigenous population. A regional drilling expert told us that if a blowout occurred late in the season, icy conditions in November and December could make well containment challenging. Shell plans to maintain an icebreaking vessel at each drilling site to conduct ice management operations, but these conditions could still pose a challenge to well containment response.

- *Ice scouring.* In addition to ice that can accumulate on the surface of the ocean, in shallow waters, floating ice can scrape along the surface of the seafloor. This has the potential to damage the wellhead and blowout preventer, as well as other well containment equipment on the seafloor. Shell representatives told us that Shell will place the wellhead and blowout preventer in a hole on the seafloor to prevent damage from ice scouring. However, this does not eliminate the possibility that the capping stack or other equipment placed on or above the seafloor, such as dispersant systems or risers, could be obstructed or damaged by floating ice.

Logistical challenges include the following:

- *Limited infrastructure.* Shell officials told us that they will have self-sufficient, dedicated subsea well containment capabilities situated on vessels in the Arctic seas during drilling operations. Nonetheless, these officials told us that additional personnel would be needed to

---

[28]As part of Interior's conditional approval of Shell's exploratory drilling plans for the Chukchi Sea, Interior will not allow drilling beyond September 24, 2012, for any drilling activities that could penetrate an area with oil and gas.

respond to a subsea well blowout. Moving personnel to the site could delay a response, since harbors, airstrips, and hotels necessary to support personnel are limited in number and size along Alaska's northern shore. The facilities are also generally much farther from the drilling sites than they are in the Gulf of Mexico, and harbors and airstrips have much less capacity to move and support response personnel.

- *Lack of redundant vessels and equipment.* According to Interior officials, because of the low rate of offshore production in the outer continental shelf off Alaska compared with the Gulf of Mexico, there is not an established industry in Alaska to manage subsea oil production or respond to a subsea blowout. Therefore, the availability of vessels and equipment to provide additional support to respond to a subsea well blowout may be limited. For example, we reported in October 2010 that U.S. Coast Guard infrastructure and assets for Arctic missions are limited, including by fuel capacity, distance to fuel sources, and crew rest requirements.[29] Shell representatives told us that the company plans to have two concurrent drilling operations capable of providing mutual assistance, but there are few additional resources available in the region to respond in the event that Shell's capabilities are insufficient.

Because Interior has not seen or evaluated Shell's well containment plans and other required documents, it is too early for us to evaluate Interior's oversight of oil and gas development and well containment capabilities in Alaskan waters. However, the existence of different types of risk and the limited response infrastructure pose additional challenges Interior will have to address to conclude that it is providing sufficient oversight.

Conclusions

Since the *Deepwater Horizon* incident, Interior has strengthened its oversight of the oil and gas industry's ability to respond to a subsea well blowout, and industry has responded by improving well containment capabilities and creating dedicated well containment organizations. Interior is developing and documenting oversight processes, and in some cases has established time frames for completion. For example, while

---

[29]GAO, Coast Guard Efforts to Identify Arctic Requirements Are Ongoing, but More Communication about Agency Planning Efforts Would Be Beneficial, GAO-10-870 (Washington, D.C.: Sept.15, 2010).

Interior has not fully documented its well containment plan review process, Interior officials told us that they expect to have documentation in place by spring 2012. Interior has also not established a regular inspection process for well containment equipment listed in well containment plans, but Interior officials told us that they are developing such a process for this equipment and plan to have it in place by June 2012. Similarly, Interior does not have a documented process for monitoring the availability of equipment identified in operators' well containment plans, but Interior requires operators to list multiple and redundant vessels and equipment in their well containment plans, and Interior officials believe this sufficiently mitigates the risk if certain equipment is unavailable. The availability of redundant vessels and equipment found in the Gulf of Mexico does not exist in Alaska, however, and is something that Interior will need to consider as it receives and evaluates Shell's plans to drill in waters off Alaska. Finally, Interior has conducted two unannounced spill drills that have included a subsea well containment scenario, and Interior officials told us it will incorporate these scenarios into future spill drills. However, Interior has not established a time frame for incorporating subsea well containment scenarios into spill drills and until it does so, there is limited assurance that operators drilling in the Gulf of Mexico or other areas will be prepared to respond to a subsea well blowout.

Recommendation for Executive Action

To help ensure that operators are prepared to respond to a subsea blowout, we recommend that the Secretary of the Interior document a time frame for incorporating well containment response scenarios into unannounced spill drills.

Agency Comments and Our Evaluation

We provided a draft of this report to the Department of the Interior for review and comment. We received written comments from Interior's Acting Assistant Secretary for Land and Minerals Management, which are reproduced in appendix II. The Acting Assistant Secretary concurred with our recommendation, stating that Interior agrees that well containment response scenarios that test operator responses to subsea blowouts should be a regular element in its annual plan for unannounced spill drills. The Acting Assistant Secretary also provided technical comments, which we have incorporated as appropriate.

As agreed with your offices, unless you publicly announce the contents of this report earlier, we plan no further distribution until 30 days from the report date. At that time, we will send copies of this report to the Secretary of the Interior, the appropriate congressional committees, and other interested parties. In addition, the report will be available at no charge on the GAO website at http://www.gao.gov.

If you or your staff have any questions about this report, please contact Madhav Panwar at (202) 512-6228 or panwarm@gao.gov or Frank Rusco at (202) 512-3841 or ruscof@gao.gov. Contact points for our Offices of Congressional Relations and Public Affairs may be found on the last page of this report. GAO staff that made major contributions to this report are listed in appendix III.

Madhav Panwar
Senior Level Technologist, Applied Research and Methodology

Frank Rusco
Director, Natural Resources and Environment

Appendix I: Supplemental Information on Typical Components of Well Containment Plans

We reviewed seven well containment plans submitted by operators. Four of the plans relied on Helix Well Containment Group (HWCG) equipment and three on Marine Well Containment Company (MWCC) equipment. The equipment listed below comprises some of the key components that could be used to respond to a well blowout and were included in the well containment plans that we reviewed.

Capping Stacks

A capping stack is a device that helps cap a well—called well shut-in—to bring a well under control after a blowout.[1] It is designed to sit on top of other equipment that sits on top of a subsea well, such as the wellhead or a blowout preventer, and forms a high-pressure seal around the well. Capping stacks have a combination of gate or ram valves to block fluid flow.[2] Capping stacks also have side outlet valves that can allow for the partial flow of oil, reducing the pressure in the wellbore, if needed. For instance, if the well containment screening tool indicates wellbore integrity will not allow for a full well shut-in, the side outlet valves will be used to direct flow to the surface capture vessels as necessary.[3] In this scenario, a procedure known as "flow and capture" could be used to partially flow the oil to a surface vessel for processing and transport.[4]

The technical features of all capping stacks designed and developed for the Gulf of Mexico are similar and made from pre-engineered components commonly used in the oil industry. Capping stacks typically feature multiple rams for redundancy. Some stacks are rated for well pressures up to 15,000 pounds per square inch (psig) and can operate in water depths of up to 10,000 feet. Capping stacks vary somewhat in height but are generally about 30 feet tall and weigh approximately 100 tons.

---

[1] "Well shut-in" refers to closing a valve to stop or isolate the flow of fluid from the wellbore.

[2] Gate and ram valves are mechanisms that shut off flow within a pipe. A gate valve incorporates a sliding gate or wedge to open or block fluid flow. A ram valve is similar in operation to a gate valve, but uses a pair of opposing steel plungers or rams that extend toward the center of the wellbore to restrict flow or can be retracted to permit flow.

[3] Well integrity is compromised if oil broaches from below the seafloor to open water.

[4] "Flow and capture" refers to the case where an operator cannot demonstrate that full wellbore integrity will be maintained by shutting in the well using a capping stack. In this case containment can be approved by Interior only if the operator can adequately demonstrate capping, flow back, and collection capability.

In response to *Deepwater Horizon,* the global oil industry formed
initiatives and advisory groups to design and develop capping stacks.
Capping stacks that are ready for deployment include the following:

Table 1: Capping Stacks Developed by the Oil Industry

Capping stack owner and region of operation	Shutting device type	Pressure rating(psig)	Water depth rating (feet)	Cap and flow capability (yes/no)
Marine Well Containment Company (for use in the Gulf of Mexico)	Single ram capping stack	15,000	10,000	Yes
Helix Well Containment Group (for use in the Gulf of Mexico)	Dual ram capping stack	10,000	10,000	Yes
	Dual ram capping stack	15,000	10,000	Yes
Wild Well Control (for global use)	Both dual rams and a single ram	15,000	10,000	Yes
Oil Spill Response Ltd. (for use in the United Kingdom Continental Shelf)[a]	Ball valve	15,000	10,000	No

Source: GAO analysis of information provided by capping stack owners or operators.

[a]Oil Spill Response Ltd. is a collaboration of seven major oil industry-funded spill response
organizations and the United Kingdom whose mission it is to harness cooperation and maximize the
effectiveness of oil spill response services worldwide.

Other Containment Devices

Other containment devices, including top hats, caissons, and cofferdams,
are used to collect or contain the flow of oil from the wellhead when a
capping stack cannot be connected, such as when a secure seal cannot
be achieved. A top hat provides a low-pressure seal and allows for a
limited collection of oil. A top hat is typically a temporary measure used
while the operator is evaluating or preparing alternative options. A
caisson creates a soft seal with the seabed—similar to a top hat—by
covering the damaged blowout preventer. A cofferdam provides no seal
to the seabed or the damaged blowout preventer.

Hydraulic Control System

A hydraulic control system is used to operate subsurface equipment, such
as to close rams on a capping stack.

Subsea Debris Removal Equipment

Debris removal equipment, such as shears for cutting pipes and remotely
operated vehicles, is used to remove debris from around a well, such as
pipes that have fallen to the seafloor following a blowout. In the event of a
blowout, debris may need to be removed to access the blowout preventer
and riser system to install the capping stack.

Subsea Utility Equipment

This equipment consists of a seafloor distribution system for injecting hydrate inhibitor chemicals and dispersants directly into the flowing oil to suppress hydrate formation and disperse the oil.[5] Multiple vessels are needed to transport and deploy these chemicals.

Well Containment Riser Systems

Risers used for well containment consist of tubing that enables access to an offshore well for emergency intervention. These riser systems allow the oil flowing through the side outlet lines of a capping stack to be routed to the surface for collection and further processing. Risers are used when operators determine that it is not safe to completely shut in the well because of the potential to compromise well integrity. In this instance, risers are attached to a capping stack, after which the well may be killed from the top—known as a top kill—by funneling mud through the risers and down into the wellbore.[6]

Support Vessels

These vessels include oil capture vessels; support vessels, such as those needed to deploy the capping stack; remotely operated underwater vehicles; and oil storage facilities. According to MWCC and HWCG, during a flow and capture procedure, these vessels are capable of handling up to 60,000 barrels of liquid and up to 120 million standard cubic feet of gas per day.

Well Kill and Abandonment Procedures

These procedures seek to successfully kill the well without compromising the well's integrity.[7] If the well's analysis determines that its integrity would be intact under top kill conditions, then the top kill option is generally used. However, if the operator determines that a top kill may cause surface broaching, flow and capture is used while the operator

---

[5]Hydrates are crystalline, ice-like compounds composed of water and natural gas. Hydrates can hinder deepwater oil production and transportation by plugging flow lines. The conditions that tend to promote hydrate formation include low temperatures and high pressures.

[6]The term "kill" in the oil industry means to stop a well from flowing or having the ability to flow into the wellbore. Kill procedures typically involve circulating reservoir fluids out of the wellbore or pumping higher-density mud into the wellbore, or both.

[7]Interior officials explained that drilling a relief well is the most reliable means to kill or plug a well because the relief well is designed to intercept the blown-out well near the bottom of the wellbore, where the source of the blowout exists

evaluates options for drilling a relief well to permanently kill the well.[8] The well is then plugged with cement and, once the wellbore pressure indicates that the well has been killed, the capping stack and blowout preventer are removed to the surface.

---

[8]A relief well is a well drilled near and deflected into a well that is out of control, making it possible to bring that well under control.

Appendix II: Comments from the Department of the Interior

 **United States Department of the Interior**

OFFICE OF THE SECRETARY
Washington, D.C. 20240

FEB - 9 2012

Mr. Frank Rusco
Director, Natural Resources and Environment
U.S. Government Accountability Office
441 G Street, N.W.
Washington, D.C. 20548

Dear Mr. Rusco:

Thank you for the opportunity to review and comment on the Government Accountability Office (GAO) draft report entitled, *OIL AND GAS: Interior Has Strengthened Its Oversight of Subsea Well Containment, But Should Improve Its Documentation* (GA0-12-244). The draft GAO report includes one recommendation for the Secretary of the Interior that is intended to ensure that offshore operators are prepared to respond to a subsea blowout. More specifically, the GAO's recommendation directs Interior to document a timeframe for incorporating well containment response scenarios into its unannounced spill drills.

The Department of the Interior (DOI) concurs with this recommendation and agrees with GAO that well containment response scenarios that test operator responses to subsea blowouts should be a regular element in its annual plan for unannounced spill drills. Within DOI, the Bureau of Safety and Environmental Enforcement (BSEE) Oil Spill Response Division (OSRD) has the responsibility for planning and conducting unannounced oil spill drills. As noted in the draft report, OSRD has already conducted and evaluated two unannounced spill drills that incorporated scenarios for well containment.

The DOI also agrees with GAO on the importance of properly documenting the standards, criteria, and procedures that will be applied in reviewing and assessing well containment plans submitted with applications for permit to drill. As noted in the draft report, BSEE plans to finalize the documentation in 2012. In the interim, BSEE has taken several steps to help ensure a consistent, repeatable review process for well containment plans that provides reasonable assurance that they are presently being consistently reviewed. Our enclosed comments provide further detail on this process.

Further, as GAO concludes, Interior has taken several steps to strengthen its oversight of the oil and gas industry's ability to respond to a subsea well blowout. In addition to issuing new guidance on the information operators must provide to demonstrate well containment capabilities, DOI initiated the development and implementation of a well containment screening tool. This tool helps DOI and operators evaluate whether a well

could be closed using a capping stack and still maintain wellbore integrity. Interior is
pleased to learn that industry representatives who met with GAO validated the utility and
effectiveness of this tool. The tool helps assess the risks associated with a subsea
blowout by requiring operators to document their well design decisions, which Interior
can then review.

BSEE is proud of its collaborative efforts and quick responses in the development of a
well containment program to improve the safety of deepwater drilling operations and the
effectiveness of potential oil spill response in the Gulf of Mexico. Based on these efforts,
BSEE's new program is regarded as a global model, and BSEE has assisted other nations
upon request.

We appreciate GAO's suggestions for improving the regulatory oversight of subsea well
containment capabilities. In addition, for your consideration, technical comments are
enclosed. If you have any questions, please contact John Keith, Chief, BSEE Office of
Policy and Analysis, at (202) 208-3236.

Sincerely,

Marcilynn A. Burke
Acting Assistant Secretary
Land and Minerals Management

Enclosure

Appendix III: GAO Contacts and Staff Acknowledgments

GAO Contacts	Madhav Panwar, (202) 512-6228 or panwarm@gao.gov Frank Rusco, (202) 512-3841 or ruscof@gao.gov
Staff Acknowledgments	In addition to the contacts named above, Bill Carrigg, Assistant Director; Christine Kehr, Assistant Director; David Bennett; Antoinette Capaccio; Nirmal Chaudhary; David Messman; Alison O'Neill; and Kiki Theodoropoulos made key contributions to this report.

GAO's Mission	The Government Accountability Office, the audit, evaluation, and investigative arm of Congress, exists to support Congress in meeting its constitutional responsibilities and to help improve the performance and accountability of the federal government for the American people. GAO examines the use of public funds; evaluates federal programs and policies; and provides analyses, recommendations, and other assistance to help Congress make informed oversight, policy, and funding decisions. GAO's commitment to good government is reflected in its core values of accountability, integrity, and reliability.
Obtaining Copies of GAO Reports and Testimony	The fastest and easiest way to obtain copies of GAO documents at no cost is through GAO's website (www.gao.gov). Each weekday afternoon, GAO posts on its website newly released reports, testimony, and correspondence. To have GAO e-mail you a list of newly posted products, go to www.gao.gov and select "E-mail Updates."
Order by Phone	The price of each GAO publication reflects GAO's actual cost of production and distribution and depends on the number of pages in the publication and whether the publication is printed in color or black and white. Pricing and ordering information is posted on GAO's website, http://www.gao.gov/ordering.htm. Place orders by calling (202) 512-6000, toll free (866) 801-7077, or TDD (202) 512-2537. Orders may be paid for using American Express, Discover Card, MasterCard, Visa, check, or money order. Call for additional information.
Connect with GAO	Connect with GAO on Facebook, Flickr, Twitter, and YouTube. Subscribe to our RSS Feeds or E-mail Updates. Listen to our Podcasts. Visit GAO on the web at www.gao.gov.
To Report Fraud, Waste, and Abuse in Federal Programs	Contact: Website: www.gao.gov/fraudnet/fraudnet.htm E-mail: fraudnet@gao.gov Automated answering system: (800) 424-5454 or (202) 512-7470
Congressional Relations	Katherine Siggerud, Managing Director, siggerudk@gao.gov, (202) 512-4400, U.S. Government Accountability Office, 441 G Street NW, Room 7125, Washington, DC 20548
Public Affairs	Chuck Young, Managing Director, youngc1@gao.gov, (202) 512-4800 U.S. Government Accountability Office, 441 G Street NW, Room 7149 Washington, DC 20548

Please Print on Recycled Paper.

www.ingramcontent.com/pod-product-compliance
Lightning Source LLC
Chambersburg PA
CBHW080932290526
45795CB00007BA/2717